You Are Not Alone

Poems of Hope and Faith

To Bob
a good friend
Love Ya
Lon Cole

By

Lon Cole

Brown and Sons Publishing
Denver, Colorado

You Are Not Alone: Poems of Hope and Faith

Copyright © 2013 by Lon Cole

ISBN 13:9780615799827
ISBN 10: 0615799825

Revised April 2013

Brown & Sons Publishing
Denver, Colorado
http://brownandsonspublishing.com

Acknowledgements

This collection of poems resulting in a book comes directly out of the support and belief of many people who encouraged me along the way: First, I want to share my deep gratitude for my family. Cris Cole, my wife, is truly my rock, my son, Alonzo and daughter, Heidi, and their families, who love me unconditionally. You all inspire me each day to share my thoughts and feelings through poetry.

My thanks to John Sharify and Doug Burgess from KING 5 Television, who shared my story with a broad audience and helped viewers to see Alzheimer's through different eyes.

Thanks are also due to two great friends: Roger Donaldson, who is a whiz at the computer, and Dr. John Davis, who has been a great support at all times.

I'd also like to acknowledge the Alzheimer's Association and my friends there, Anita Souza, Keri Pollock, and Bob Le Roy. Thank you for asking me to share my verse and tell my story, along with opportunities to serve as a volunteer partner. Thank you for your support on this journey.

And last, but certainly not least, I want to send a big thank you to my fellow early stage memory loss support group members, whom, more than anyone else, have a deeper, more personal understanding of what I express through my poetry. I am proud to be part of our collective voice.

My great appreciation to Brown & Sons Publishing, and in particular to Dr. Jocelyn A. Brown, who was enthusiastic about this book, took on the role of editor and publisher, and has helped me to realize a dream.

Lon Cole

TABLE OF CONTENTS

Introduction

Inspired by his own unique experiences, Lon has kept records of his life in poetry and writing. Being an artist myself, I have truly admired his ability to express his emotions through his writing. It's never easy to convey feelings, and yet he does so with such ease in his words. Each poem is like a window into a piece of his soul that has been far overshadowed by the daily strength that he must demonstrate. I have come to learn, as you will after reading this book, that all of us can be taken to the depths of despair. All of us can be wounded, yet it is within us to rise from it and become stronger. Word after word, he continues to surprise me, as he so effortlessly portrays the most basic human emotions. From joy and peace to fear and loneliness, his poetry touches on the emotions that unite us all.

Even now, after being diagnosed with the terrible disease of Alzheimer's, he has found a way to buoy up those around him. After reading this work you will know that you are not alone. His most powerful voice will be the one you will hear as he connects with you through poetry.

Without question, I know that his poetry, his attitude, and simply his presence among those who suffer from this disease, directly and indirectly, are strengthened by him.

It is an honor to be his daughter. Life will give to all of us what we need to grow stronger, and he has taught me that our very purpose on this earth is to love our families and our fellowman and to enjoy every minute of this life!

Heidi Grace Kress
April 2013

Foreward

My father was diagnosed with Alzheimer's disease fifteen years ago this week. He's 97, a slight, gentle, confused man, near—but not yet at—the end of a long and well-lived life. But what about those whose journeys with Alzheimer's disease and related dementias are just beginning? Who will be there for them with help and hope as they struggle to cope with their uncertain and unwelcome futures?

No one personifies the diligence and determination, energy and effort, heart and humor of our early stage outreach quite like Lon Cole. Lon and his wife, Chris, attend an early stage support group. He serves on our Early Stage Advisory Council and our Pierce County Regional Advisory Council. He is a peer-to-peer counselor. He is our Chapter's poet laureate!

Lon's poetry is truly the window to his soul. In *You are not Alone*, he opens that window for all of us, guides us through heartache to hope, reminds us what we mean to one another and of our better selves, and leaves us feeling "*alive and thankful*".

Three of Lon's poems have special meaning for me:

"My Partner" is a valentine to a life partner. I shared it with my wife on our wedding anniversary two weeks ago.

Now you're with me always
Wherever I may go
The love that we both honor
Will fill my lonely soul

"Where Am I Going?" urges us to hold tight to the gift of life.

I'll look for tomorrow and live for today
And hold to the good as it passes my way
I'm strong to the challenge and must be sincere
For life is a gift, so precious and dear

"The Visions We Share" is a life-affirming response to growing old.

The visions we share are simple today
That is because we need them that way
You're only as old as your heart wants to be
So live all you can and learn to be free

Lon honors us with his poetry and his service. I'm proud to say that he honors me with his friendship. At the Alzheimer's Association, we offer help and hope. Our vision is a world without Alzheimer's disease. With partners like Lon, we are in very good company.

At the Alzheimer's Association Western and Central Washington State Chapter, we are taking steps to engage and serve this emerging and rapidly growing early stage population. "Early stage" refers to people, irrespective of age, who have been diagnosed with Alzheimer's disease or related dementia and are in the early stages of the disease. In this stage, individuals retain the ability to participate in daily activities and give-and-take dialogues. This group includes individuals with "younger onset" Alzheimer's—under age 65 and still in the early stages of the disease.

One of the key objectives in our current strategic plan is to "be an early and ongoing point of contact for people diagnosed with Alzheimer's disease, either directly or through a caregiver". To achieve this objective for persons with dementia and their care partners, we:

- Added an Early Stage Memory Loss Coordinator to our staff to engage and serve our early stage client base utilizing a "best practices" approach to integrate elements of successful programs currently in use across the Association

- Host eight early stage support groups

- Recruited an early stage advisory council of persons with dementia and their care partners to guide us in the assessment, development, and enhancement of our early stage outreach

- Launched a "peer to peer" program linking trained volunteers with dementia to newly-diagnosed individuals for ongoing education and support

- Collaborate with the Frye Art Museum on the "here:now" program of arts engagement

- Collaborate with Seattle Parks and Recreation on a weekly walking program at the Woodland Park Zoo

Bob Le Roy
President and Chief Executive Officer
Alzheimer's Association
Western & Central Washington State Chapter

You Are Not Alone

Poems of Hope and Faith

As We Forget

Are we forgotten as we forget
Do we lose all that we are
Or is it a dream that never ends
Just memories so distant and far

We reach, we grab for a moment in time
It slips by us ever so slow
Some will tell us you're losing your mind
The difference we never will know

Where is the truth we actively seek
And search for the answer so clear
It lingers beyond our growing hopes
And relinquishes all of our fear

The answer is near and so plain to see
The puzzle so easy to solve
Just keeping the faith will make us all free
To let God intervene with his love

Demented

When will it darken
Either day or night
My eyes are wide open
Where is my sight

How can I touch you
If I don't know the way
Why did you leave me
You promised to stay

Who do I hear now
Where do I go
Was I just there
Does anyone know

I have a question
The answers are not there
Does anyone hear me
Are there people who care

The light is still fading
I will lose what is mine
No one to help me
My soul cannot shine

Discovery

Anger was my focus
When answers were not there
What I wanted was solutions
And to be with those who care

I was buried in my fear
Not understanding why
Though you saw me smiling
My heart would often cry

I showed a different side
Of what I wished to be
A soul that's trapped from inside out
That longs to be so free

Then the answer came to me
In such a simple way
To live your life the best you can
And celebrate each day

Each Step We Take

Traveling down a long lonely road
May seem like no one cares
When someone helps you carry the load
The trip is light to bare

Each step we take if on our own
The journey appears undone
There is no need to cry or moan
Together you are more then one

Do not fret if another is near
To lend you a helping hand
Be thankful for the one so dear
Who will truly understand

No matter where you go or where you have been
Our Lord is always there
To help you have the strength within
Your burdens he will share

Faith And Beyond

Faith is the anchor for the soul
It follows us wherever we go

Losing a loved one is an awful plight
But when faith comes along things turn out all right

God has a way of steering you straight
He mends what you have lost, and carries your weight

Things aren't the same. I guess that's okay
For God is in control, and will show us the way

The ones that we love who are gone from our sight
Some day will return to brings us new light

Faith - A True Course

Faith is such a special word
It rings with strength and peace
And gives to each one of us
A hope that will not cease

Sometimes life seems all so dark
The road is marred with haze
It passes by us ever so quick
And leaves us in a daze

But faith makes our path crystal clear
Our journey is straight and true
It opens the doors that are usually closed
And the old and forgotten become new

Believing is a way of life
No one can mar the course
For truth will prevail and always win
When the Lord becomes our source

Forever

When you're pulling down the shade of life
Try not to suffer from worry or strife

Those that you love are not far away
The ones who passed on get closer each day

They seem to be saying in a soft tender voice
That where you end up is a matter of choice

The life that you live is hard to foresee
Each step that you take will help make you free

Be wise in your living whatever you do
And make life an adventure until it is through

You won't be forgotten, there's so much to see
Your eyes will be open to all of eternity

Having a Shadow

Sometimes life is like having a shadow
That follows every step that you take
At first it seems like honor
But in time all you want is a break

You need your own space, a place all alone
But your shadow denies what you seek
It wears you down and tires your soul
And your spirit also becomes weak

It's time to realize why your shadow is near
And remind you of its darkness and fears
The burden you bear is a lesson to learn
The light that you give erases the tears

Hold On

If you're the one who gives the care
Your challenge is strong and may seem unfair
You must endure what comes your way
And hold your ground as they're slipping away
Be there to listen as long as it takes
And be able to give though your heart wants to break
Cherish the time with those that you love
Hold to the memories and pray to above
Be strong if you can, life will go on
Don't lose your hope when your love one is gone

Hope Is Near

Don't give in whatever you do
Hope will always be there for you

If your challenges seem hard to bear
Remember that the Lord will always care

Hope can be a way of life
It battles the anger, and conquers the strife

So when you are struggling you need not to fear
For where there is hope the Lord will be near

Believe and trust in all that is true
You won't be alone no matter what you do

Give hope a chance, it never will fail
And hold your ground, for good will prevail

I Served My Country Well

I served my country well
I did my time in hell
I fought the battle we all did lose
Without the drugs, without the booze

Why did we die, why did we bleed
Was it for power or was it for greed
And now our country wants to forget
The sacrifice of the Viet Nam vet

Someday war will come again
What could we tell our sons
What honor could we promise them
When they see what we have done

How sad and lonely they will feel
As they march off to war
With stories of the older vets
Who fought in vain before

So now I tell America
From me and all my friends
Who gave their arms, legs, and lives
So freedom would never end

Life Is A Special Gift

Life is such a special gift
That brings us joy and peace
But sometimes things aren't so good
That's when pain and suffering increase

It's how we really live our life
That determines which way we sail
Doing our best is the final test
A test we must never fail

Surviving all the storms of life
Must be our truest quest
The effort that we all put forth
Has to always be are best

Be not afraid, but face your fears
For God will help you win
The victories that you have in life
Has truly has no end

Life Gets Tougher

Life gets tougher everyday
It seems like a puzzle that is hard to play
No matter how much or how we complain
We lose much more then we ever could gain
It's like a big battle that will never end
And all of the troubles come again and again
Our goals, they seem hollow and beyond what we know
The paths, they get longer and move ever so slow
Is there an answer, a way we can win
Or is it a huge circle that has no end
I must believe a solution is there
And surround myself with all those who care
No matter how complex my troubles may be
There is always another who will be there for me
I know there is help wherever I go
I hold to the steady and blessings will show
One by one the good will prevail
No matter what happens I know I won't fail
I count every blessing, so precious they shine
I learn to be thankful and open my mind

My Partner

I can still remember
As far back as can be
The memories that I treasure
Are the ones of you and me

We loved and laughed together
Each moment was a gift
A precious treasure always
That gave my heart a lift

Yesterdays are fading
Before today appears
When I seek the answers
I find my recent fears

All I know is nothing
Now it's all so still
Are you there to help me
My empty mind to fill

You are there to show me
I must take your hand
Time is quickly passing
Will I understand

Now you're with me always
Where ever I may go
The love that we both honor
Will fill my lonely soul

So Close to Your Heart

Those that we love are so close to our heart
We cling to their memories as they slowly depart

We want to do something that will keep them close by
While looking for comfort we want to know why

Why are they leaving when we want them to stay
How can we help them while they are drifting away

Hold to the good times and know how you feel
Each moment is precious and ever so real

Keep living your life the best way you know
And hold to the rod and never let go

As your day arrives and it is your time to leave
They will honor your memory and always believe

The Moment is Now

The moment is now
The future is near
I cannot forget
And try not to fear

Whatever I see
Wherever I go
Life seems so fast
Why can't it be slow

Things just pass by
I reach but they're gone
I would like them to stop
But they always move on

A thought or a memory
Confused every day
Where are the answers?
Will I find the way?

I must not forget
That while memories are shot
There is more to my life
Then what I forgot

To Be a Tree

The mighty tree, it stands so tall
The lonely man, he looks so small
I hope and pray that I could be
So tall and strong and sway so free

But I am just a lonely man
Who walks along the lonely sand
And dreams of mountains and skies so blue
And a giant forest with clear lakes so cool

He sees no war, this giant green
No auto wrecks or man-made machines
Dear God, I dream and pray I will see
When all mankind is like my friend the tree

What Is Real

Giving care is not an easy task
Especially for those unaware
Quite often your feelings are masked
In an effort to show that you care

Each moment of time spent on another's behalf
Brings peace to your troubled soul
It opens your heart where your feelings are trapped
So emotions and love can flow

A tear or a smile, they both mean the same
An effort to show how you feel
This giving of oneself is more then a game
In serving, you will discover what's real

Where Am I going

Where am I going, will I ever get there
Will somebody know me, does this all seem fair

I'm sure there is someone who feels what I feel
But has trouble expressing the pain that is real

But I must keep going and steer from the past
For each day is hopeful, and nothing is cast

I'll look for tomorrow and live for today
And hold to the good as it passes my way

I'm strong to the challenge and must be sincere
For life is a gift, so precious and dear

You Are Not Alone

I have been told that you're not alone
I wish it was always that way
So often it seems you're on your own
They leave when you want them to stay

You search for the right answers
But even the questions are gone
You rest for a moment or two
But all your worries still move on

The quest, it seems so shallow
As the victory is slipping away
Solutions, they are too hollow
There is darkness even at day

I am not afraid to face it
I must do the best that I can
And if I fall short in my journey
I will get up and start again

Friends

True friends are here to stay
They give much more than they take away

They know how to listen when you need them to
Their words are wise, and usually true

They won't leave you when the chips are down
When the road is rocky they will still be around

Real close friendships will last for a life
And you are very lucky if they're your husband or wife

If you lose a friend, the pain is deep and long
When you gain a friend you feel happy and strong

A friendship is a two way street
To be a friend makes the circle complete

My Quest Never Ends

I search for the answer, my quest never ends
And hope to be valiant in the battle I must win

I will call for my champions and conquer my fears
And triumph with valor as my time nears

I will look past the darkness and kneel as I pray
I must look for the question as I ponder each day

And when I'm convinced that truth will prevail
I will give thanks to God for he never will fail

Smile

The gift of a smile can brighten our day
It raises us upward and colors the gray

A smile is the sunshine each person can show
It warms all our spirits, and gives light to the soul

It requires some work when you're sporting a frown
To create a smile is much harder then it sounds

When you live with a smile you can truly take pride
For all those that see you will be happier inside

Sunday Again

Yes, it is Sunday again
And to church we all will go
For it's been a very long and hard week
And there's so much to learn and know

Yes, it is Sunday again
And it eagerly awaits the Lord
For us to enter into his house
And pray and worship to his accord

Yes, it is Sunday again
It fills our hearts as we sing
To honor our Lord Jesus Christ
Who is creator, redeemer, and king

Yes, it is Sunday again
And the meeting has come to a close
We will climb in our cars and head for our homes
With the spirit of the Lord in our souls

There Was a War

If in this land
There was a war
And son fought
Hard and was slain
Along with grief
I would share some pride
To know that he died
Not in vain

But he died in a land
So far far away
From all that I loved
And once knew
And the Lord
I do say, will
Hear what I pray
And will let my poor son
Come though

It matters not
Where he may be
Or how he
Was taken away
His time in my life
Was such a great gift
A treasure, a memory
That will stay

Challenge

I like a challenge every once in a while
It sharpens my senses and improves my style

It helps me wake up to what life is all about
To be alive and thankful, I just want to shout

Thinking outside the box is a way to find peace
It helps me be stronger, my knowledge will increase

It teaches me lessons beyond what I can see
It opens my mind and sets my soul free

Not every challenge will help me succeed
But victories are priceless, a triumph indeed

So when a great challenge stumbles my way
I trust in the Lord to hear what I pray

Prayer To Above

Prayer is a way to speak to the Divine
It's a chance to share what's in your heart and mind

When you pray to above you show that you care
You hope for the answer and have faith it is there

Praying is not a one-way road
We must carefully listen in a spiritual mode

The answers may not be what we want them to be
They will be right and they will set us free

How long and when should we pray
A prayer in your heart every moment of the day

You don't want to pray for others to see
Pray in secret and on your knees

Resume' Of The Heart

I am still here, where else could I be
Life is a struggle, but its worth it to me

Some days are dark, and others bring light
Sometimes I feel awkward, some days I'm just right

One thing I know, life is a gift
It gives us meaning and our heart a big lift

I may not be the same as I used to be
Memories could fail, but you can always trust in me

I may be a little rusty in some things I know
But I can learn quickly, and I never work slow

Sometimes I'm wrong, I'm the first to admit
I won't make excuses, I'll just get right to it

If I forget to show up one day
Just send me packing, I'll be on my way

Believe in me as I do in you
Together there is nothing we can't do

Show That You Care

See the glow on your face and the smile in your eyes
Show the world who you are and why you are wise

When you laugh from your soul there is much you can share
So never be afraid to show that you care

The kindness you have carries joy in your hands
Your wisdom bows to all it commands

The work that you do equals the service you give
You teach us all how to share and a better way to live

Your absence of fear is a sign of your courage
You're easy to trust and you don't get discouraged

But most of all, is to feel all of Gods love
That happens to be His gift from above

Waiting In Line

Waiting in line can be such a pain
While others move forward I still remain

How long will it take, I'll be here all day
It's driving me crazy, how long must I stay?

Please call my number before I go mad
Why is everyone staring at me? Do I look that bad?

I can't even remember why I got in the line
If I don't get out of here I will lose my mind

Somebody cut that's, not fair to the rest
I'm tired and angry at the whole stinking mess

"Closed for Lunch," what's happening to me
I think I am losing it, what else can it be?

I'm out of here, I can't wait anymore
I will come back tomorrow, but it's such a great bore

We All Need To Laugh

Its good to make fun of yourself now and then
For telling a good joke is never a sin

We all need to laugh as often as we can
It clears our minds and helps us to understand

The physics of laughter is an interesting sight
It's good for the body, both day and night

Laughing will help when you're in pain or depressed
It erases the worries and gives your body a rest

So let out a laugh and see what it can do
I'm sure you will feel better and not have the blues

Early Stage

There's a middle aged man just standing around
He looks confused and a little bit down

He just came from a store and is straining to see
He's wondering where his car might be

He has a bad memory when he has to recall
And struggles with crowds, especially the mall

It's hard to accept that he no longer drives
That he has to depend so much on his wife

He tries to do the best that he can
To give all whom he meets a helping hand

Middle Stage

Trapped in between the darkness and light
Is a little old man alone in the night

He doesn't remember like he used to before
Trying to talk becomes a great chore

He walks very little, there's nowhere to go
When asked if he'll join us he always says no

He wears the same clothes, it's so hard to change
When he's in a crowd, he feels very strange

There's not much more I could say about him
Except the light in his soul is beginning to dim

Late Stage

I hear a voice call out to me
A weak little sound is all it can be

Trapped inside an old tin can
Is what is left of a once young man

Where does he go when he can't find the way
He's covered in darkness on a bright sunny day

Now he is quiet, he can no longer talk
He rides in his chair, forgets how to walk

He hears very little and can't reply
A little bit of life still twinkles in his eye

He stares into emptiness he can hardly see
But someday that old man will finally be free

The Pain Never Stops

Pain is a feeling we all have to bear
There are all kind of pain, it's hard to compare

When I'm hurting deep down inside
That's the worst kind of pain, I must confide

It seems like forever, the pain never stops
You're hurting so much that your heart wants to drop

You're left on your own, confused and depressed
You call out for help, but your mind is so stressed

Physical pain you can't often recall
Emotional pain makes your skin want to crawl

The best way to deal with the pain that I feel
Is to share it with God as I bend down to kneel

He helps us be free from all kinds of pain
It rests on his shoulders as peace we obtain

The World Is Getting Smaller

It's such a crazy world out there
People mixed up that don't seem to care

Their actions are unusual I have to say
Some should be committed and carried away

Others could be quite normal, it's hard to tell
Lost in a darkness, they aren't doing very well

Wanting for answers, confused by replies
Not understanding and still asking why

How can you reach them, are they all lost
We must try to help no matter the cost

Everyone feels a little crazy now and then
Failing to help them is truly a sin

The world is getting smaller, it's different each day
The changes are gigantic in every way

Where Do We Go

Sometimes our memories come and go
They pass through our minds, fast and slow

We try to hold them as tight as we can
We end up confused and don't understand

Where did they go? Why are they gone?
Will they come back or have they moved on

Most memories we lose are short term I'm told
It usually happens when we start getting old

"I can't remember" is a familiar phrase
Our minds end up in a dark misty maze

It's happening more often, I'm afraid to say
We seem to forget something every day

Where do we go to get help that we need
Someone that's wiser than me, I concede

Whoever we find must really care
They must have our trust and be willing to share

A Dream Or Two

Everyone has a dream or two
You must be determined for it to come true

When you have found what you're looking for
Your quest is not over there is so much more

Give it your all, do your best
Pick up your pace, there's no time to rest

You have to work hard to discover your dream
There's so much to do, much more then it seems

Finish your journey, then your mission is complete
Remember the taste of victory is always so sweet

A Family With Love

What makes a family be who they are
If they are united their love will go far

Treat each other the best that you can
Give more then you take, learn to understand

Being a father is hard to explain
It's more than the work or the money you gain

A father's duty is to protect and provide
Be there when he's needed with arms open wide

A mother is special in so many ways
She nurtures and cares for her children each day

When both work together the family does great
The children are happy and each pulls their weight

This seems like a dream that almost could be
But a family with love is a treasure to see

A Great Journey

Dementia is a great journey
Where too many have to go
You can't try to run from it
No matter how much you know

Some say denial is the way
To avoid the pain you endure
Others decide to face it straight on
They hope there might be a cure

It doesn't matter if you're rich or poor
Or have several degrees on the wall
What matters the most is your attitude
Getting up each time that you fall

You can't be afraid of what you might face
The road could feel lonely or cold
Though you are only one of the human race
This is the time to be bold

Celebrate survival the best way you can
Remember all the good times you had
So when the dark days come into your path
You won't waste your time feeling sad

Death Or Life

Death is an adventure we all have to face
There is no option for the whole human race

Death for so many is something to fear
Especially when it is getting so near

Life is a choice we learn to explore
It's what we pursue whether rich or poor

Some say that death has a loud voice
I feel that both are something to rejoice

For life is a gift we all must get through
Death is a beginning of something that's new

Death is not so dark but yes, it is real
Life brings you light so you can feel

I'm not in a hurry to meet death at my door
I'll take life though it's hard to endure

God Only Knows

When life is lost, there's a special cost
Where money can never go
Each person gone still lives on
inside of another's soul

The pain is real and can't heal
No matter what someone does
They strain their eyes and often cry
When they're thinking of who it was

Remember this,you'll always miss
The memory of one you loved
But in your mind you will find
God's peace that comes from above

So where we go God only knows
It's strictly a matter of choice
The closer we get, we have to admit
Its time for us to Rejoice

A War Of Hurt

I stared into the emptiness
To find my way again
My eyes were wandering everywhere
In hope the curse would end

The feeling of depression
Is hard to push away
It holds you tight in its grip
And haunts you night and day

How do I deal with sadness
That dominates my mind
There are drugs to take and books to read
That helps my brain unwind

I mustn't give into the pain
Or lose the battle within
Just free myself of how I feel
And the war of hurt will end

A Witness From Above

I remember that special day
When Christ was born in a humble way

We sang joyful songs throughout the land
To proclaim to the world the Lord is at hand

We watched our Savior learn and grow
Into a man the whole world would know

Far above we heard Him speak
Of loving your neighbor and blessing the meek

The sick were healed, the crippled could walk
Thousands would follow to hear Him talk

But so quick, His mission was nearing its end
And we knew His great suffering would soon begin

We cried as He wept in the garden that night
As the spear pierced His side, it was a sorrowful sight

We watched as they laid Him in a tomb cold and gray
But three days quickly passed and the stone rolled away

For God showed His glory in a powerful way
The son of God has risen on this easter day

Our Father now reigns with the Lord at His side
Resurrection is a promise to all who will and have died

Anger Is A Feeling

Anger is a feeling we must endure
It comes and it goes, this is for sure

Learning to deal with the anger we feel
Is a trait we must achieve, for anger is real

Some say that anger can do you some good
Stay in control, don't be misunderstood

Learn not to fight every time you are wrong
Say that you're sorry, then just move on

Don't let your anger get the best of you
Just swallow your pride and keep your cool

Believe In Yourself

Sometimes life appears to be a dead end
You don't have a job, you've lost all your friends

You feel all alone, you have forsaken your church
Something is missing despite your hard search

When you reach the moment when it seems all is gone
That's when you know you just have to push on

Don't give up easily, you must hold on to win
You're not alone, you're in a place we've all been

It's not over till you give up the fight
You can't quit now when hope is in sight

Things will get brighter as we approach the day
Something will happen so life goes your way

Faith is the answer to your plight
Believe in yourself, it will turn out all right

Bow Into The Wind

When your troubles of life begin
Just turn your bow into the wind

Facing your problems is a better way
It will help get you through every day

Life is a challenge for all to bear
Conquer your worries, discover your cares

You can't run away from what you feel
Concerns won't leave because they are real

Be strong if you can, you're not here to lose
Stand up for your freedom, it's your right to chose

Don't try to escape from strife you ensue
Because when you do, they will still chase after you

Creation

Mother nature is our best friend
She's always around and will never end

All of the animals have their own place
Plant life surrounds us and fills its own space

Creation is a gift that shines from above
The beauty is amazing as He shows His great love

The earth, sun, and stars have no end
I can see forever, where does it begin?

I witness eternity as I look up in the night
For life continues even beyond my sight

God is the maker of all that we see
He is our creator and sets us all free

Darkness Will Follow

I'm not afraid to stare into fear
Especially when I'm not on my own
When someone else is by my side
I'm stronger than when I'm alone

I won't remember most of the things
That I was scared of before
That's one of the blessings Alzheimer's brings
There're others that I have to explore

Darkness will follow the years as they pass
I fear I will get that emptiness stare
Void of desire to learn what's new in my life
I suspect that I won't even care

Trophy and awards I used to achieve
Are covered with dust on my wall
My new life is simpler indeed
The successes I have now must seem small

Dignity

To lose one's dignity is a really big deal
You're losing yourself and all that's real

It's like you've been kicked in the back or behind
Or you have been told you're losing your mind

Treat all with respect and dignity, too
Someday the finger may be pointed at you

If someone is sick or covered with flaws
Don't make it worse, no matter the cause

Give them a smile and a handshake
Look in their eyes and a friend you will make

Fear

Fear is a feeling we all have to face
Don't run from your fears, you won't win the race

Everyone gets scared quite often, we know
The fear that we feel may come and go

It's what we do when the fear's in our way
Do we face it straight on or do we let it stay

There is something good when we face all our fears
It develops a strength that lasts through out the years

When you are scared and fear starts to flow
Just stand up straight and let your fears go

Fitness

Being healthy is the right thing to do
It lengthens your life by a decade or two

Staying healthy is a lot of work
Don't take it lightly, but don't go berserk

Exercise often and eat the right foods
Be a positive thinker, maintain the right mood

Don't throw in the towel when you're feeling low
That is the time when you can't let go

Strive to be fit, work at it each day
It will all be worth it, you must not delay

Always remember, take care of your health
The value is priceless, far greater then wealth

Give Daily Care

It must be a challenge to give daily care
Day after day you must always be there

When you get tired, how do you rest
You have to have someone who will give it their best

Caregivers are a rare, special breed
They care and love you and see to your needs

Care for someone close in your life
Most often it will be a husband or wife

Time is your foe, each trial you must face
You have to keep going till you finish the race

And if you fall down you must stand up again
A day will arrive when it comes to the end

It may be a sad day, a day of great pain
But you gave it your best with nothing to gain

The one that you served may have moved on
But the love that you shared will never be gone

Goals

I truly wonder about setting new goals
They're always the same and don't come from the soul

Lose lots of weight and exercise more
Pick up the mess that's spread on the floor

Goal after goal, when will it stop
It's driving me crazy, my brain wants to pop

Maybe a few goals I'll chose at this time
I've got to do something, I'm losing my mind

I guess I'll just change the date on the goals from before
That's plenty of goals I don't need anymore

Beauty Surrounds Us

The children play around the stream
In a land so fresh and green
The mountains stood high and reached for the sky
Their summits could hardly be seen

The trees are tall and rarely fall
The animals run wild and free
The air is clean, sweet and pure
A beauty as far as can be seen

This land we love could soon be gone
The peace and quiet we will miss
And in its place a manmade world
All void of loveliness

But now the nature surrounds my soul
And follows me wherever I go
How great that God made these wonders to see
And dwell within us for all eternity

A Hard Wooden Floor

Once I went to the old country store
I wasn't doing much, my life was a bore

I met an old man I had never seen before
He was dancing the jig on the hard wooden floor

I asked him his name as he continued to dance
He stared right at me as if in a trance

I asked him again as I let out a yelp
I looked at the others who offered no help

And finally he spoke just one single word
He answered "why," how strange and absurd

I had enough from this coy little guy
I hollered so loud and let out a cry

"What is your name, I won't ask you again"
He calmly answered back "why" as he continued to grin

That's all I could take, I now had enough
Now he would see that I could be tough

I hit him right square, then I hit him once more
But I swear he was still grinning as he fell to the floor

Now it was just he and I on that hard wooden floor
Then a little old lady walked through the door

She looked at me with pain in her eyes
And let out a scream, "why, oh why"

What could I say, I just lost my cool
The answer was senseless, I felt like a fool

Then the old man stood up and still had his grin
But I had given him a bloody nose and a cut on his chin

She came over to comfort him and started to cry
Again she cried out "why, oh Why"

At that moment I realized what I had done
I beat up an old man that was just having fun

"What is his name," I asked, as she carried him by
His name is Wyatt but we just call him Wy

I am not having fun, my life's still a bore
As I'm setting in jail on a hard wooden floor

He's Now In Heaven

I miss my Dad, he's been gone for a while
He always knew how to make me smile

On Friday we would often play cards and
He was always willing to help in the yard

He said he was lonely since Mom was gone
In his house there was always a TV left on

He fought in two wars, a sailor was he
When I got my own medal he was so proud of me

He's now in heaven with Mom at his side
Just waiting for us with arms open wide

I'll Never Regret

I'll never regret the day we first met
I hope that you feel the same
You're the only one that I truly loved
I'm glad you carry my name

We were very young and leaned on each other
To get through the troublesome days
Two individuals on the same path
We held together in so many ways

We're getting a little bit older now
And wiser in our advancing years
So when things sometimes get tougher on us
We're not swallowed up by our fears

Stay by my side as long as you can
How quickly the future goes by
Together there is nothing that we cannot do
As long as we give it a try

In the Mirror

I looked in the mirror, I stared so deep
Who is that person who has started to weep

Do I know him, is he a friend
He seems to be troubled, and alone again

Will he be lonely the rest of his life
Does he have someone, maybe a wife

I wonder why I can't remember his name
He looks so familiar, I'm going insane

Someday I'll ask him why he just stares
He is so stoic, and seems not to care

Well I have to go now, that's all I can say
Maybe I'll see you some other day

Love the Lord

Did you live the life the Lord gave you
Are you now on the real course
Have you wasted the precious time you have
Do you recognize the true source

You must pass the test that you were given
If you want to go to the head of the class
You won't be graded by how many you failed
Or even how many you passed

What determines your score for today
Is the effort that you put in
To show how you honor the Lord
As you triumph over your sins

Don't get discouraged or low
Just do all you can do
The Lord intercedes in so many ways
He's there to help get you through

So discover the life that he gave you
A brilliant life it will be
Learn to love the Lord in every way
You'll then know how to set yourself free

Made in The U. S. of A

Where is America, where has it been
Is it the same country we used to live in

What's made in America is always the best
American-made will pass every test

Some things have turned upside down
When you look for the best it's never around

Where can we go, what can we do
Everything's cheaper for me and for you

What do we stand for, how can we know
Is made in China the best we can show

We better wake up before it's too late
For our children's sake we really can't wait

We must get back to made in U.S. of A.
Or our rights and freedoms could be taken away

Memories Of Childhood

Children like to play and have lots of fun
They laugh and they giggle in the brightly lit sun

They like to discover things that are new
They're usually honest and talk straight with you

Alone, they get nervous, that's how it can be
Together with others they jump and run free

My memories of childhood were the best times of all
We could play all day with one little ball

Then, when it was time to go inside
Mom would be waiting with her arms open wide

We were all very lucky we didn't need much
With hamburger helper and mom's magic touch

Now that I'm older life is so complex
We don't talk to each other, now we just text

Worried

When you are worried you can never let go
You're haunted, you're scared and it bothers your soul

You cry out to all as you wipe away tears
It drives you crazy and loads you with fears

You're covered with questions, the answers you seek
Can somebody help you, the mind's getting weak

Clear answers would help in so many ways
Worries can linger and go on for days

Where is the clarity you desperately need
We must solve the troubles we have, to succeed

When the worry is over you feel great relief
You can say goodbye to sorrow and grief

P.T.S.D.

Fear rocks my soul every night
I can't let things be, I'm wound up so tight

The thoughts in my mind are weirder than me
They scare me a lot and won't let me be

The pills that I take subdue all my harm
I'm luckier than most, I won't cause alarm

I'm haunted by warriors that won't let me go
They call out to me and reach deep in my soul

The dreams are the worst, I have to say
I'd sleep much better if the dreams went away

I puzzle my brain, is there hope for me
All I can hope is to someday be free

Shadows Of Life

The shadows of life are usually dark
Trouble and worries appear
You search for the way to erase the thoughts
The memories grow into fear

Sometimes it feels that it's all a bad dream
You will wake up and just feel fine
While you're awake you'll search for the answers
That are locked up deep in your mind

Finding the key that unlocks the brain
Is as hard as the key to your heart
When both are open a mystery is solved
And then believing will start

There lies the hope your soul can now feel
No matter how dark it had been
Now you're prepared for whatever comes
With peace you find from within

Joy is the conqueror of all that was lost
The victory so sweet and so pure
Free from the shadows that linger too long
Your spirit and body endure

Stress

Some days you feel like you're ready to blow
You're so anxious you can't even think
You're all tied up in one big knot
And your spirit's beginning to sink

Why does the body react in this way?
There must be some pill you can take
Is it a feeling or physical pain
You feel like your body will break

You're feeling so tense you just want to shout
You pray that it will not stay
You're hurting so much you want to cry out
You'll do anything if it just goes away

You're down on your knees asking for help
You figure there's no where to go
You've taken the pills, you listened and talked
And finally your heart starts to slow

The nightmare is over at least for tonight
The sun shines brightly and clear
The battle subsides it was a good fight
Your soul is filled with good cheer

Without Any Work

When you're without work you have little pride
You feel so desperate, you wish you could hide

A person needs work to move them along
Without a job things turn out wrong

There are people who really want a career
They will study and learn and go anywhere

They're not here to joke, make fun, or play
They just want to work hard throughout every day

The Elder

I met a young man awhile ago
Whose spirit seemed to shine and glow
The words he spoke reached deep inside
Far past my fear, my doubt, and my pride

The water was warm as I rose from the fount
A joy filled my heart, what more could I want
The gift of the Holy Spirit was bestowed upon me
My eyes were opened, my soul was now free

I've learned so much since the day that he spoke
Of truth, wisdom, faith, and hope
I've made commitments to serve and obey
To forsake all my sins, to study and pray

It's still a great challenge, a battle I fight
But now I have knowledge and I chose what's right
If I follow the Lord as long as I live
I will walk in his presence, my sins he'll forgive

Now those I meet and those who I know
All seem to say that I shine and I glow
I share my sweet secret in hopes they will see
That they can have joy and make themselves free

Winning is Great

Winning is great when you're on the winning side
Doing your best brings you true pride

Victories are measured by the work you put in
Each time you fall down just get up again

Effort is equal to energy spent
I'll tell you a secret, I'll give you a hint

You give all you got then you give a bit more
You'll feel the triumph and spirits will soar

A champion is someone who'll never quit
They'll keep running when they just want to sit

Treat everyone equally, don't act like the best
Prove that you're great by acing the test

Be a good sport in all that you do
Shake hands with all when the contest is through

The Journey

I took a look deep down inside
Far past my guilt, worries, and pride

The deeper I went the more painful it was
Will I get past the pain or discover its cause

I continued my journey exploring my thoughts
Way past the battles my mind often fought

I might understand what's bothering me
If I just go deeper, I'll set myself free

Then it just happened like opening a door
So fast I was moving, much deeper than before

My mind had gone the deepest it's been
The suffering was over, the pain will now end

My spirit was free, how clear I could see
A glimpse of the heavens was open to me

The sweetness of peace filled my soul
This was my quest, this made me whole

We're On The Same Path

When you're disabled you struggle each day
To live your life in a normal way

Those who can't walk, hear, or see
Are still the same as you and me

We live on the same planet and breath the same air
They're not asking for more, just to be fair

If we can help all that we can
It makes it easier to live in this land

We're on the same path to a better life
Together we'll conquer our worries and strife

The Son

The Father, The son, and The Holy Ghost
Are the supreme beings of us all
Adam and Eve were the start of the race
They were the very first humans to fall

The Son's mission was to redeem all mankind
To free us all from a spiritual doom
He sacrificed Himself and took on our sins
Three days later He rose from the tomb

He guides and counsels us with His love
No greater love there ever could be
If we obey Him and hold to the course
We will live with the Lord and be free

His life was an example of how we should live
The lessons He taught were ever so pure
If we could follow down the path that He led
We'll soon make it to heaven for sure.

Trust In The Lord

The challenges of mortality never cease
You face them every day of your life
We live to find each day of peace
We're surrounded by worries and strife

We call on the Lord to rescue us
From problems we seem to find
We search for the answers to bring us peace
And to ease our troubled minds

The love of the Lord fills our souls
With a calmness we often seek
Temptations may soar beyond our control
And trap us when we become weak

Faith is the answer that sets us free
Believing when we need to know
Delight in our God will help us be
Able to achieve all of our goals

We'll become stronger when we trust in the Lord
The mind and heart will unite
Our prayers will be answered to His accord
And the wrongs may be conquered by right

Springtime

This is a special time of the year
Things change right before your eyes
The colors become so vivid
The clouds open up from the skies

The sun it shines more often
And the cool air starts to warm
The animals become more active
And the mountains change there form

Spring has so much to offer you
The streams are crystal clear
The melting snow feeds all of life
And brings nature also near

The grass it looks much greener
The trees they sway so free
You can hear the sounds of everything
From a waterfall to a buzzing bee

The smell of spring is amazing
There's so many smells to enjoy
Just take a deep breath and soak it all in
There's no need for you to be coy

Be thankful for what we're given
And the special time of spring
So if we listen carefully
We can hear mother nature sing

Show Us The Way

Where can we go when the road looks dark
What do we do or say
Will we be lost in deep black night
Will anyone show us the way

Sometimes life gets too hard to bear
We search for the answers, unclear
And when we find all that we seek
We will face it with courage, not fear

Is our journey a lonely road
Or will we find help from the light
It glows on the path to show us the way
It helps us to know if we're right

The shadows we see may limit our hope
Beware of the mist in the air
We'll gather our course and follow the Lord
For without Him we're lost in despair

Celebrate Survival

There are all kinds of problems that drag us down
But there is always a way to turn them around

We live to be happy which helps us to live
But there is no true happiness until you learn how to give

Discouragement is a word that we learn how to fight
The opposite is accomplishment, which is doing what's right

So celebrate survival in the best way you can
And honor all of life because living is grand

Be fierce in your battle in doing what's good
Don't waste your time on being misunderstood

Be alive and be thankful for all you can be
Count your very blessings and be glad you are free

Darkness

Sometimes life can get very dark
It preys on you like a man-eating shark
Your mind goes blank, it's called a stupor of thought
And when you wake up your brain is all shot
Add a cup of depression and you got yourself in a mess
This happens to me often, I have to confess
Nothing seems clear, you're dumbed into a maze
You struggle to exit but everything's a haze
Where is my clarity, why am I so lost
I have to do something no matter the cost
Maybe I can meditate and hope to get out
I am so tied up that I just want to shout
Where is the peace where can I go
There must be a place where calmness will flow
Sometimes my writing helps me endure
The shadows brighten and I feel all so sure
A deep breath or two will show me the way
I'm glad that it's over, the night turned away

Live To Be Free

In our country we live to be free
And to be whatever we want to be

We're taught to be the best that we can
That we are unique whether woman or man

If we work hard there's nothing that we can't do
Discovering our dreams is what we pursue

It doesn't matter if we're strong or meek
What matters the most is the truth that we seek

The knowledge we find may be our reward
But we should always remember it came from the Lord

Then get on our knees to say thank you
For believing in God is the right thing to do

Mother Nature

I looked into the sky one day
To see what Mother Nature had to say

Look at my greens, look at my blues
Such pretty colors I offer to you

Be still my friend don't say a word
And you will hear the chirp of a newborn bird

For I am here to help you feel free
And soak in the sweetness as far as you see

Stretch To The End

We can't win every battle we fight
Losing happens sometimes in life
It is what we do when we lose
How we deal with the pain and the strife

There's a part of me that says just go on
Have the faith it will all work out
But the other part wants to push me down
I will get angry and just want to shout

I must endure and not lose my dream
I must realize its within my reach
If I just hang on a little bit longer
I will gain the wisdom that I seek

Don't throw in the towel or call it quits
When you are within reach of your goal
Hold to the rod and stretch to the end
Have faith in your self and your soul

Without Reward

Giving is an act of love
That the Lord would always do
When we give without reward
Our blessings are never through

Where, when, or how we give
Is not as important as why
In giving all that we can in life
It's worth more than money can buy

Everyone needs to help in some way
In doing so your spirits will climb
Helping others who can't help themselves
By giving money, talents, or time.

You should honor your service
By giving as much as you can
Whatever you give is worth more than you have
There is joy in lending a helping hand

Volunteers

Volunteers have such a noble career
They're givers that serve us ever so dear

Without them not much would ever get done
They work for the many and give to the one

Where would we be without them today
Their service is worthy in every possible way

They have a great gift they are willing to share
You are a better person whenever they're near

So reach out and give without a reward
The time is well spent and you will never be bored

Truth Will Prevail

Believe all you can that truth will prevail
For no matter what happens you're not here to fail

Your life is so precious beyond what you know
And when you're confused it's hard to let go

Try not to be selfish, learn how to share
For God's special gift will always be there

Help others who need to find their own way
And always remember to pray every day

Pray in the morning, pray every night
The answers you get will always be right

The Visions We Share

To be young again is a dream come true
We learn as we age that life isn't new

We get tired more easily than we did before
When we were in a hurry, and lived to explore

Now time is so precious, we pay a high price
We dream of the days when all was so nice

The visions we share are simple today
That is because we need them that way

You're only as old as your heart wants to be
So live all you can and learn to be free

Nine/Eleven

Thousands of Americans died that day
It happened so quickly, they were taken away

I was at home watching it all
My body was weak, my mind hit a wall

So many people, martyred and slain
We can't let their memories go down in vain

Something then snapped inside of me
I need to go back and serve my country

I know I'm too old but what can be done
I'll pray for our warriors to protect everyone

This dishonoring deed made by men far away
Will be avenged, I pray to hasten the day

A Brighter Day

My day is brighter when you come my way
You lighten my burdens and gladden my day

When you are gone I wander about,
When you are with me, my heart wants to shout

I may not remember all that you do
But the time that we share carries me through

Please stay by my side as much as you can
Your strength, we will share as we walk hand in hand

Alzheimer's

Tell me a disease that has no end in sight
It can take you by day or the middle of night

This deadly illness has no cure
It doesn't matter if you're rich or you're poor

It's a modern day plague that must be stopped
Or the toll it takes will go over the top

Those who battle it are few in ranks
But they deserve all of our thanks

It can be conquered, that's for sure
Together we can, its been done before

A Medic's Call

It's just an old story that I'd like to share
A story of joy and a story of fear
A story told through a young man's eyes
It might make you smile or might make you cry

Deep in the jungle, in the middle of war
There's this 19 year old boy who has been there before
A shout for a medic rings out through the air
The young man gets up and starts to prepare

He knows his duty despite his great fear
To help rescue someone, for all lives are dear
He's shot pretty bad, what should I do?
Then another explosion, right next to you

The sting of the metal, the burning hot pain
Then in comes another and stings you again
You're weaker now then you were before
You must do something before there is more

I must help my friend, but what can I do?
Just let out a scream, others will help you
Finally there's someone to take your friend
But sadly they're unable to come out again

Now it's just you, you're all on your own
Bleeding, in pain, you're all alone
You must make a run before it's too late
Your chances are slim, but there's no time to wait

A dash through the bullets everywhere
Just keep running, you might make it there
Finally, somewhere they can't shoot at me
I'm still alive, but where could I be?

Here comes my rescue, a small little man
I'm carried to safety as he holds my hand
Now I'm safe from all of this war
Friends head back to the jungle to look for some more

A Special Gift From Above

Be thankful for your blessings
They're a special gift from above
He's only there to help you
To shower your life with His love

A blessing can be eternal
Far beyond compare
You're never quite alone, my friend
The Lord has much to share

Each morning that you breathe fresh air
The dreams from night now end
A new day is here for the world to see
Life's adventures start again

The day is done, you approach night
Did it go as well as it could?
Or was it a day you'd like to forget
A day without much good

Blessings come when you need them
Have you learned to make them stay?
You must count your blessings everyone
Give thanks to God each day

Cold As Ice

The wind is blowing'
The air is cold
It chills my body
Right to my soul

How can I warm
The inside of me
A roaring new fire
Or a pot of hot tea

Though I'm freezing
Right to the bone
I'm sure to find
I'm not on my own

The love from a friend
Can warm me inside
There's no need to fear
And nothing to hide

So though my body
May be cold as ice
The warmth from my heart
Makes everything right

Death And Beyond

Death comes to us in many ways
In many shapes and forms
Some say death can be very cold
Others say it's warm

In truth it's a change of address
A time for souls to be free
The body will rest for awhile
But soon unite for eternity

Death's not final, but all-inclusive
All will experience this event
It takes us all in our due time
Something no one can be prevent

But that's all right, it's not that bad
Unless we act with fear
Though your loved ones seem far away
In truth they're ever near

No one really wants to die
We deny it as long as we can
When the time comes, the Lord's in control
He'll be there to take your hand

Together you'll walk through the Vail
The light, as bright as the sun
You'll be with family and friends
You'll know and love everyone

You won't be idle at this time
There's so much work to be done
But you won't get tired like before
You'll feel good and bless everyone

Don't Stand Alone

Share the burdens we all carry
To lift the weight from our souls
Help us find the humble way
To conquer troubles we know

Worries can be a heavy weight
Loading you down with pain
Find a way to free yourself
There is so much to gain

Don't stand alone in the work you do
Remember who is by your side
The Lord will always be there for you
With His arms opened wide

You won't fail in your mission
To free you from the strife
The Lord is here to save you
He'll be there throughout your life

You need to just hold your ground
Especially when you feel low
Be there for those who love you
Your faith will make you whole

Driving With Others

To drive a car equals independence
The choice to go where you can
Along comes responsibility, liability
May make you change your plan

What do you do when it's no longer safe
To drive your car anywhere
How hard it must be to hang up your keys
To show other drivers you care

Some say it's safe to drive just a little
As long as it's to a familiar place
How do you decide how little is too far
Not everyone has the same case

If you're driving because you can't let it go
Think hard before you decide
Are you doing what's best for others
Or is it just a matter of pride

Choose wisely my friend as you get in the car
Which side you'll sit on today
Will you be cautious and safe for others
Or let reason be thrown away

Example Of Christian Love

One day I looked out the window
A surprise was waiting for me
My neighbor was working in my yard
How blessed could a man ever be

It was an example of Christian love
That we all should try to pursue
He taught me a lesson I needed to learn
That the Lord would always do

He gave all he could to his fellow man
Including his life so free
That we might learn to live like him
And give help to all we might see

My neighbor is really a good example
Of how a Christian should act
I know if the Lord did ask him
He would give the shirt off his back

Where can we go, what could we do
To show our love for the Lord
We could live like he would want us to
And learn to worship by His accord

He Will Set You Free

Dementia is a serious disorder
It attacks the brain and has no borders

Your memory leaves and nothing remains
All you're left with is a dying brain

It just isn't fair how it picks who will die
If you're wealthy or smart, it won't pass you by

The older you get, the higher the chance
What can you do now, you must take a stance

Wherever you go, whatever you do
Trust in the Lord, He'll be there for you

You can get through this, you can put up a fight
Laying down, giving up, just isn't right

Keep the door open, do all that you can
Life is worth living, you just need a plan

Plan for the future, be all you can be
Show faith in the Lord, He'll set you free

I Need To Be Free

You're traveling on a peculiar trail
Each step you take, something new is unveiled

Then you come up against a great wall
The first thing you notice is the wall is too tall

You look to the left and then to the right
It keeps on going far out of sight

How will you get to the other side
That is a puzzle, you must confide

If only the wall had a way to get through
You could continue your trek toward all that is new

Suddenly you discover a transparent door
It's very strange that you'd never seen it before

The trail keeps on moving on and on
Far past the door, the wall, and beyond

The path still gets better beyond what you see
But the door is locked and you don't have the key

Then you realize what's in store for you
You cannot move forward no matter what you do

You call out to the Lord, "I need to be free"
Please help me God, I must find the key

Then the door opens all on its own
Your eyes stop crying and your heart ceases to moan

The trail is now clear for you to move on
Now all your worries and troubles are gone

You've discovered what eternity truly can be
It's never ending, you'll forever be free

The Gift of Life

When you're fighting a fatal disease
Your spirit can become worn
Nothing seems to lift you from the dark
You wish you were never born

There is an answer to all that you feel
Your soul just needs a great lift
So when you pray very hard
The Lord will provide you a gift

What could this be in such a hard time
How can you ever feel good
You need a clue of what you must do
What have you misunderstood

Life is a gift as long as we live
We all share the beautiful earth
We are never alone, we're so close to home
He's been with us way before birth

When you feel God's love inside
Your life is complete once again
Be at peace with all that you do
The truth is, life never ends

It's just a change of address
There's still much more to see
Your old tired body is taking a rest
So the spirit can soar and be free

Life Is A Journey

I want to help everyone that I can
To look to the future and think life is grand

To rid themselves of the pain of before
To find the strength that helps them feel sure

Sure of the hope of a bright sunny day
That good will happen as you move on your way

Life is a journey we all must endure
With hope, we can live a life that is pure

Enjoy the gift that a good life can bring
Always give thanks to the Lord our great king

When life comes to an end you can say with great pride
I tried to live my life on the right side

Nothing To Fear

Climb aboard, the trip is free
Don't be afraid of what you might see
Open your eyes as wide as you can
Try to remember and to understand

Where are we going? I'd like to know
Somewhere new I really hope so
You count the people who are coming along
I'll be the tour guide and sing them a song

Song of discovery, a new tune we hear
We're just having fun there's nothing to fear
When do we get there? I really hope soon
It's getting darker, I don't see the moon

My eyes are wide open there's such a bright light
I feel so at peace, it all seems so right
So many people, I know everyone
I can't believe it - it's bright as the sun

They are all smiling and looking at me
I've got to go further, there's so much to see
I feel so at home in this wonderful place
Since God is near I can feel His grace

I think this is heaven, I hope that it is
There's no pain or sorrow only pure happiness
Thank you for coming with me my good man
It makes me so happy to be together again

Out Of Synch

Sometimes the heart isn't in tune with the brain
Confusion and heartbreak is all that remains

Where do you start to make the repairs
Both are essential, they both need good care

Neither can function all on it's own
They both would fail if left alone

The spirit is the glue that helps them unite
When they're working together everything's right

The mind needs its peace, the heart needs its calm
If they team up together, they create a strong bond

So when the mind and heart are out of synch
You'll forget how to feel and be unable to think

Pain

Pain is a feeling that can last a lifetime
It seems like it will never go away
It's there to remind us how the body works
There could be a pain for each day

There're all types of pains we all know well
A pain to the body and a pain to the soul
Our pains can be treated with all kinds of pills
But pain to the soul is hard to let go

Sometimes we abuse the pain pills we take
That can create pain to the mind
It's like a whirlwind that spins 'round and 'round
Or like a large spring trying to unwind

But the pain in your soul goes ever so deep
And stings you from inside out
It'll make you depressed as you long for relief
It erupts in loud angry shouts

You find yourself pleading for help
From friends and those whom you love
You even drop to your knees with a humble request
Seeking guidance from God up above

There's no way to know how pain will fall
But it's easy to know that it will
So trust in the Lord who took on all your pain
Sacrificing his life on that hill

Reason To Hope

Do you have a reason to hope?
Or is it beyond all you can bear?
Are you staring into the darkness?
Do you feel like no one cares?

Go back to having hope again
It will help you conquer your pains
Without it you are probably lost
Faith in yourself cannot be sustained

Hope equals faith in so many ways
It gives you a chance to survive
You are put right on the front steps of God
It helps you feel you're alive

Don't lose your hope, keep it close by
You'll need it when times get bad
Hold yourself steady, lean on the Lord
Especially when you're feeling sad

Believe in yourself, you won't be let down
You didn't come to earth to fail
Nobody said it would be easy for you
But hope will help you prevail

Regrets

When you have regrets
You're living in the past
Life becomes a do over
Because your die is cast

So many times in life
I regret the things I've done
How hard it is to say you're sorry
For every single one

Give me a second chance
To correct the mistakes I've made
File them past my mind and heart
In one long single parade

If I could make the corrections
That would ultimately change my course
I could be free of all the pain of regret
That's followed by so much remorse

So give me new hope
To make what was wrong a right
Resolution is what I seek
Put the misery out of my sight

I must not forget
To repent for all of my sins
So if I am forgiven
I can never do it again

Still Seems The Same

Grandchildren are a blessing for us all
They come in all sizes from large to small

They help your day go very fast
The energy they generate will give you a blast

They're easy to spoil, they brighten the day
And when they're gone they're missed right away

They make you feel younger, though they can wear you out
They never stop thinking as they move all about

When it is time to say goodbye
The hardest thing is to watch them cry

When they get older they still seem the same
They move a bit less but live up to their name

Life would be boring if they weren't around
That's why I look forward to hearing their sound

To the Caregiver

Sometimes a sickness seems too hard to bear
Because you need help doesn't mean you don't care

Caregivers do the best that they can
When that's not enough they need a helping hand

Bring in the help your loved one will need
It may be a health center that takes over the lead

You still need to be there for the one that you love
Hold tight to the answers that come from above

Some decisions may be hard to make
And sometimes the answers are real hard to take

Do what you trust in is the best way to go
The Lord will be with you, He'll help you to know

Alive and Thankful

Some days are good days
Some days are bad
I want to be happy
I want to feel glad

If I could remember
Like I used to before
And treasure those moments
That made me sing and soar

The names and the faces
I knew everyone
And now they're a puzzle
Each memory is gone

I haven't forgotten
How to laugh or to cry
Or say I'm alive and thankful
When someone walks by

Things aren't so bad
They could probably be worse
But I count my blessings
And consider the Source

Lon shares reflections on his diagnosis of younger-onset Alzheimer's, being "Alive and Thankful," and his poetry with a new audience, April 2013. *Photo Credit: Mike Bonn*

Reason to Hope Breakfast, Tacoma, April 2013. Bob Le Roy, President & CEO, Alzheimer's Association; Alonzo Cole, Jr., Lon's son; Cris, Lon's wife; Lon; Heidi Grace Kress, Lon's daughter; Lon's granddaughters; John Sharify, Event Emcee and Emmy-winning KING 5 Television reporter, who told Lon's story in the 2012 documentary, "Alive and Thankful." *Photo Credit: Mike Bonn*

John Sharify, Emcee, introduces Lon, keynote speaker at the Alzheimer's Association's Reason to Hope Breakfast in Tacoma, WA, April 2013. *Photo Credit: Mike Bonn*

Lon's first Emmy Award, taken at the 50th Annual Emmy Awards, Seattle. John Sharify, reporter, KING 5 Television; Keri Pollock, Communications Director, Alzheimer's Association; Doug Burgess, photojournalist, KING 5 Television; and Lon holding the Emmy for Writer-News, Sharify Stories, "Alive and Thankful", June 15, 2013. *Photo Credit: Team Photogenic*

John Sharify, Reason to Hope Emcee and KING 5 Television reporter; Lon and Cris Cole, Lon's wife. April 2013. *Photo Credit: Alzheimer's Association, Western and Central Washington State Chapter*

One of Lon's granddaughters was at the Reason to Hope Breakfast. *Photo Credit: Mike Bonn*

Author Outreach

Lon Cole serves as an Alzheimer's Association Volunteer Partner in several capacities:

Early Stage Advisory Council (ESAC)

As a member of the ESAC, Lon's role is to direct the focus of programs and services established specifically for individuals and families affected by younger-onset Alzheimer's and other dementias. The ESAC is responsible for the programming of the Early Stage Memory Loss Forum, an annual educational conference that addresses topics specific to the needs of those in the early stages of dementia.

Pierce County (WA) Regional Advisory Council

Pierce County (WA) Regional Advisory Council is one of nine councils across western and central Washington State created to identify and meet the needs of individuals and families affected by dementia in those counties. Input from members about what they are seeing and hearing in their communities relative to needs, perceptions, and potential donors and partners is the essence of the councils. They are the eyes and ears of their designated regions, helping to reach more people in more places.

Peer to Peer Program
Lon is also a trained Peer-to-Peer Outreach Advisor. The Peer-to-Peer program connects newly-diagnosed individuals with trained persons in the early stages of Alzheimer's or related dementias to provide an empathetic ear as well as a unique perspective based on their experiences and their knowledge of the Alzheimer's journey. Participants can speak candidly and confidentially with a person who understands what the newly-diagnosed individual is going through.

Documentaries
Title: *Alzheimer's A Journey of Love*
Copyright 2013 Lively Productions
Focus: Alzheimer's and how to approach the journey with grace and love.
We follow 4 stories in different stages of Alzheimer's. Esteemed
neurologists and geriatric care managers join us and a few other surprises.
Documentary will be completed December 2013 and air in 2014. For more
details on how to get your copy visit www.livelyproductions.net
100% of net proceeds go to the South Sound Alzheimer's Council and
STARS.

Title: *Alive and Thankful*
2012 SCCTV, KING5
Seattle Washington
Focus: Lon Cole and Early Onset Alzheimer's
Winner of the Regional Emmy Awards, June 2013

Title *Wandering*
Airdate: Monday, July 22
KCTS 9 (Seattle PBS station)
Supplementary website includes a link to the full documentary, as well as
excerpts from the piece. http://kcts9.org/wandering

Resources

Alzheimer's Association
www.alz.org
800.272.3900
Alzheimer's Association has a 24/7 Helpline. You can call at any time of the day or night and get advice and information about Alzheimer's and other dementias and about the many issues and challenges of care giving.

National Institutes of Health
www.nih.gov/
NIH's mission is to seek fundamental knowledge about the nature and behavior of living systems and the application of that knowledge to enhance health, lengthen life, and reduce illness and disability.

Area Agencies on Aging
www.n4a.org/
202.872.0888
By providing a range of options that allow older adults to choose the home and community-based services and living arrangements that suit them best, AAAs give older adults the opportunity to remain in their homes and communities as long as possible.

Veterans Administration
www.va.gov/
800.827.1000
The VA administers a variety of benefits and services that provide financial and other forms of assistance to service members, veterans, and their dependents and survivors.

Alzheimer's Association TrialMatch
www.alz.org/research/clinical_trials/find_clinical_trials_trialmatch.asp
800.272.3900
Alzheimer's Association TrialMatch® is a free, easy-to-use clinical studies matching service that connects individuals with Alzheimer's, caregivers, healthy volunteers, and physicians with current studies.

University of Washington Alzheimer's Disease Research Center
www.uwadrc.org
800.317.5382
At the University of Washington, the Alzheimer's Disease Research Center's main priorities are to find the causes of Alzheimer's and to identify effective treatments and prevention strategies for this tragic disorder. The ultimate goal of its basic and clinical studies is to improve patient care and functioning, as well as to improve the quality of life for both patients and caregivers.

Mayo Clinic Alzheimer's Disease Research Center
www.mayo.edu/research/centers-programs/alzheimers-disease-research-center/overview
507.284.1324
At the Mayo Clinic, some of the world's leading researchers are looking for ways to predict Alzheimer's Disease, improve diagnostic techniques, identify high-risk individuals, and develop analytical tools to aid in the search for preventative treatments and an eventual cure.

Alzheimer's Association – Younger-Onset Alzheimer's Resource Page
www.alz.org/alzheimers_disease_early_onset.asp
Alzheimer's is not just a disease of old age. Younger-onset (also known as early-onset) Alzheimer's affects people younger than age 65. Nearly 4 percent of the more than 5 million Americans with Alzheimer's have younger-onset.

Alzheimer's Association
alz.connected.org
Connect with an online community that offers Alzheimer's support.

Living Your Best With Early-Stage Alzheimer's: An Essential Guide by Lisa Snyder, LCSW

A wonderful, rich, informative and hopeful resource for anyone beginning a journey into Alzheimer's or related dementia. Lisa Snyder strips away fear and negativity to roll out this road map on how to have the best life and make every day count. Highly recommended for persons diagnosed with early dementia and their friends and families. Available at Amazon, Barnes and Noble, and other bookstores.

Perspectives, edited by Lisa Snyder, LCSW

http://adrc.ucsd.edu/news.html

Perspectives is a quarterly newsletter written for people with dementia that addresses the concerns, reflections, and coping skills of individuals with Alzheimer's or a related memory disorder. It provides up-to-date research, explores relevant topics, provides a forum for discussion, and builds bridges among people with memory loss around the world. Individuals with Alzheimer's or a related disorder contribute their perspectives to this newsletter in the form of articles, poetry, or letters. ***Perspectives*** is written and edited by Lisa Snyder, LCSW and published by the University of California, San Diego, Shiley-Marcos Alzheimer's Disease Research Center. Robyn Yale, LCSW and staff of the Shiley-Marcos ADRC serve as editorial advisors.

Donating: How You Can Make a Difference

Donate to the Alzheimer's Association and help fight Alzheimer's disease through vital research and essential support programs and services. Remembering that your gift will support life and fund research, please select the type of donation you wish to make:

Honor a loved one with a one-time tribute or memorial gift.

Make recurring gifts that ensure stable funding for our vital work.

Support a Walk to End Alzheimer's™ team or participant.

Donate online:

http://www.alz.org/join_the_cause_donate.asp

24/7 Hotline:

1.800.272.3900

Donate by mail:

Send your gift check to: Alzheimer's Association P.O. Box 96011 Washington, DC 20090-6011

About the Author

Lon Cole is a man of many talents and many experiences. He was born as a bona fide baby boomer in the Bay Area of California. His father had the distinction of serving in both World War II and the Korean War. Service to his country was part of his heritage and he followed the call to serve in the Navy as a combat medic in the Vietnam War where he was decorated as a war hero for gallantry and distinguished service to his fellow soldiers. This determination to help others is reflected in the diverse and interesting career paths he has experienced, including surgical technician, police officer, private security, and a business owner and entrepreneur. His friends and colleagues know him to be a man of great wit, with a happy countenance, and absolute integrity.

Lon has faced many adversities in life from a dysfunctional childhood, serious wounds from his service in Vietnam, and many other medical difficulties that have challenged him throughout his life. He is supported by his wife of over 40 years, his two children, their spouses, and his 8 grandchildren, with one on the way. He has also leaned heavily on his unwavering faith in God and his resolve to serve Him by helping lift the burdens of others. Lon has also found strength in helping others by writing poems. It started after his challenging service in Vietnam and has continued to be a passion of his in an effort to lift up his family, friends and anyone who needed encouragement through his poetic words.

In recent years Lon was diagnosed with early onset Alzheimer's disease and has found that this challenge in his life has motivated his pen, and the poetry has flowed freely and often as he puts his feelings and efforts to lift others into his poems. Even though he has started to forget some things, his efforts to record his inspirations and thoughts have been more productive than ever. He loves to make people laugh, lift their spirits, and make them think about what matters most. Most of all, he wants people to be alive and thankful for the privileges God has given them. He currently resides in Puyallup, WA surrounded by his family.

Made in the USA
Charleston, SC
10 September 2013